combat sports

robert sandelson

OLYMPIC SPORTS

Crestwood House
New York

Maxwell Macmillan International
New York   Oxford   Singapore   Sydney

OLYMPIC SPORTS

TRACK ATHLETICS
FIELD ATHLETICS
SWIMMING AND DIVING
GYMNASTICS
ICE SPORTS
SKIING
BALL SPORTS
COMBAT SPORTS

Designer: Joyce Chester
Editor: Deborah Elliott

Cover: Lennox Lewis of Canada (left) in the super heavyweight final in Seoul against Riddick Bowe of the United States. Lewis emerged as the winner.

CRESTWOOD HOUSE
Macmillan Publishing Company
866 Third Avenue
New York, NY 10022

Macmillan Publishing Company is part of the Maxwell Communication Group of Companies.

First published in Great Britain in 1991
by Wayland (Publishers) Ltd
61 Western Road, Hove, East Sussex BN3 1JD

Printed in Italy by G. Canale & C.S.p.A.
1 2 3 4 5 6 7 8 9 10

ACKNOWLEDGMENTS

The Publisher would like to thank the following agencies and photographers for allowing their pictures to be reproduced in this book: All Sport *cover* (Gray Mortimore), 7 (Preben Soborg), 10 (Mike Powell), 12 (Steve Powell), 16 (Gray Mortimore), 19 (top, Simon Bruty), 21 (Mike Powell), 27 (Russell Cheyne), 29 (J. M. Loubat), 37 (John Gichigi), 39 (John Gichigi), 41 (right, Gerard Vandystadt); BBC Hulton Picture Library 6, 8, 9, 26, 28, 31, 42 (both); Colorsport 15, 18, 19 (bottom), 20, 22, 23, 24, 35, 36, 40, 41 (left), 44 (both), 45; Topham 4, 11, 13, 14, 17 (both), 25, 30, 32 (both), 33, 34, 43.

Library of Congress Cataloging-in-Publication Data

Sandelson, Robert.
    Combat Sports / Robert Sandelson.
        p.   cm. — (Olympic sports)
    Includes bibliographical references and index.
    Summary: Describes the history, rules, and great moments of the Olympic combat sports of boxing, fencing, judo, and wrestling.
    ISBN 0-89686-668-8
    1. Boxing — Juvenile literature. 2. Fencing — Juvenile literature. 3. Judo — Juvenile literature. 4. Wrestling — Juvenile literature. 5. Olympics — Juvenile literature.
    |1. Hand-to-hand fighting.| I. Title.   II. Series.
GV1136.S26   1991
796.8'3 — dc20   91-24685

CONTENTS

COMBAT SPORTS 4

BOXING 6

      PAPP 25

FENCING 27

JUDO 33

WRESTLING 41

GLOSSARY 46

FURTHER READING 46

INDEX 47

COMBAT SPORTS

The Olympic Games take their name from the Games that were held in Olympia in ancient Greece from about 776 B.C. Sports events were held at the altar of Rhea — the "Mother of the gods." The Games were a sports festival — a tribute to the supreme athletes of the day. All the winners received olive branches, which were symbols of vitality.

Combat sports were first introduced in 708 B.C. when a wrestling competition took place. Boxing was first competed in 688 B.C. As with other sports, the combat events were designed to test strength and skill, and not to produce bloody, vicious battles.

The Olympics were revived in 1896 in Athens, Greece, by the Frenchman Baron Pierre de Coubertin. His dream was to hold a sports extravaganza to test the skills of athletes from around the world. He believed: "The most important thing in the Olympic Games is not winning but taking part. The essential thing in life is not conquering but fighting well." Unfortunately, the Games have had to struggle to remain true to de Coubertin's famous ideal.

Combat sports have been featured at the modern Games from almost the beginning. They have always been associated with controversy and a certain amount of notoriety.

There are two conflicting philosophies of what constitutes combat within the Olympic spirit. The more basic view is that such sport is (at heart) one of rough and tumble, blood and danger. Therefore, contestants run the risk of getting badly hurt. The other

▲ The Olympics were revived in Athens in 1896 thanks to Baron de Coubertin.

view is that the combat should only be a test of skill and strength and should have little blood involved in it. Fencers, for instance, do not expect to get hurt; a mere touch — not a bloody goring — scores a point.

The second view is prevailing in boxing — contestants now wear headguards that prevent many of the cuts to boxers' faces that often used to stop fights. Judo and wrestling can both be dangerous, though today the emphasis is on skill and agility rather than overpowering an opponent at all costs.

THE IMPORTANT THING IN THE OLYMPIC GAMES IS NOT WINNING BUT TAKING PART. THE ESSENTIAL THING IN LIFE IS NOT CONQUERING BUT FIGHTING WELL.

BARON de COUBERTIN

Whichever philosophy you choose to follow, there is no doubt that combat sports remain popular events in the Olympic Games.

▲ The opening ceremony to the first modern Olympic Games in 1896. On the noticeboard is the Olympic ideal that was Baron de Coubertin's dream.

BOXING

Boxing was one of the sports contested at the Olympic Games in 688 B.C. The last recorded bout was in A.D. 369. The sport was revived at the modern Olympics in St. Louis in 1904. These Games were considered something of a disaster. It took four and a half months to complete the relatively small number of events. All the competitors were from the United States, except for a few "guest" track athletes. Few European countries took part, and even Baron de Coubertin did not attend.

Four years later in London things had hardly improved, with Britain taking all but one of the boxing medals. However, there were some talented competitors in the competition, for example J. W. H. T. (Johnny) Douglas. Although he won the gold medal, it was not without controversy — his father was the referee in the final. It is hard to imagine his being both a good father and an impartial judge in a boxing ring.

The great boxer J. W. H. T. Douglas was also an excellent batsman; he was captain of England's cricket team eighteen times. His initials allowed critics the pleasure of inventing a memorable nickname for the defensive batsman — "Johnny Won't Hit Today." If these people had seen him box they would never have called him that! Douglas was also a first-class soccer player and played for Britain's national team. As we will see, the ability to combine boxing prowess with other sporting skills was by no means unique to Douglas.

The Games in Stockholm in 1912 did not include boxing for the simple reason that the sport was illegal in

▲ British boxer J. W. H. T. Douglas boxed his way to victory in the Olympic middleweight competition in London in 1908.

Sweden! In 1920 in Antwerp, Belgium, a truly international tournament took place. The Olympic motto *"Citius, Altius, Fortius"* (Faster, Higher, Stronger) was adopted at these Games. Boxers from all over the world took part and in some cases won medals. In Olympic terms, the most famous victory was by Edward Eagan, one of the most brilliant of crossover sportspeople. Eagan is the only man to win golds in both Winter and Summer Olympic Games. In the Summer Games in Antwerp he won the light heavyweight boxing gold medal. Twelve years later he was a member of an illustrious crew that won the four-man bobsled gold medal at the Winter Games in Lake Placid. Edwin Moses, double Olympic gold medalist in 1976

▲ The "Korean incident" occurred in 1988 in Seoul. Byun Jong staged a sit-in as a protest against the judges' decision in favor of his opponent. He left when the lights went out.

and 1984, and probably the greatest 400-m hurdler the world has seen, will enter the bobsled competition in Albertville, France, in 1992, in an attempt to equal Eagan's achievement.

Olympic boxing has never been short of controversies, thrills and excitement in the boxing arena. Practically every Olympics is marked by some heated protest or other. In Seoul in 1988, a sit-in by a Korean boxer was typical of the sort of protest that boxers sometimes make against decisions they do not agree with. Contentious decisions are

J. A. Wright of Britain slips a right under the guard of H. Garcia of Argentina (left) during their middleweight contest in 1948 in London.

frequently made, and there is usually little accounting for them. In such a heated and violent atmosphere, tempers run high, and the very fact that an Olympic medal is at stake for physically assaulting an opponent makes boxing very aggressive. Fans get particularly involved in the fight and often start fights of their own, which can intimidate referees.

The most famous and bizarre of all boxing controversies was the Brousse–Mallin affair in Paris in 1924. In the quarter-finals of the middleweight contest, Frenchman Roger Brousse faced British police officer Harry Mallin. Mallin was the reigning Olympic Champion after his victory over Georges Prudhomme in Antwerp,

Belgium, in 1920. The fight, which looked to impartial observers to have been going Mallin's way, was awarded to Brousse at the end in a split decision, 2–1. Mallin left the ring and went up to the referee — the referee officiated from outside the ring in those days — and showed him bite marks on his chest. Brousse had bitten him, a crime he had been accused of in the first round. The French boxer was immediately disqualified. Brousse's supporters were outraged by the decision, refusing to believe in their hero's guilt. They tried to assault the judges and

▲ A. Diaz Cadabeda of Spain (right) defeated M. B. Shacklady of Britain in their welterweight contest in London in 1948.

were prevented from entering the ring by the police.

Mallin entered the final of the tournament the following day against fellow Briton John Elliott. Unfortunately, the fight was totally overshadowed by the protests from Brousse's supporters. Mallin's victory was, needless to say, poorly received.

Four years later in Amsterdam in the Netherlands, the controversies rained down thick and fast on the Olympic boxing tournament. The day of the finals, August 11, was a disaster from beginning to end. First, in the featherweight competition, the final, between the Argentinian Victor Peralta and the Dutchman Lambertus van Klaveren, the judges awarded the fight to the local boxer. There would have been no problem with this decision if the Argentinian had not obviously won the contest. The Argentinian supporters started to fight with the Dutch police.

The heated atmosphere was sustained by the outcome of the very next bout. In the flyweight division, sixteen-year-old Hyman Miller of the United States looked as if he had easily outboxed Marcel Santos of Belgium. At the final bell the referee awarded the bout to Santos. The American team immediately threatened to withdraw from the competition. This had no effect on the result, and the team was also refused permission to withdraw by the U.S. Olympic Committee.

As if the day had not been eventful enough, the next contest also deteriorated into a confrontation. In the middleweight bout between Piero Toscani of Italy and Jan Hermanek of Czechoslovakia, the Czech seemed to have the upper hand. The judges disagreed and awarded the fight to the Italian. The Czech supporters lifted Hermanek onto their shoulders, and violence broke out in the hall. Soon the police arrived, for the second time that day, and allowed the fighting to continue, inside the ring.

Of all the Olympic boxing events, it is the heavyweight division that attracts the most interest and media coverage. The same can be said of the world championship bouts. The Olympic heavyweight champions are usually the most memorable because of the increased attention they receive. Many people would argue vigorously that boxing is not glamorous, but few could deny that the heavyweights have added sparkle to the Olympic Games.

Heavyweight
The very first heavyweight champion was Samuel Berger in St. Louis in 1904. By turning professional immediately after the competition, he set a pattern that was to be repeated in the future. However, using the Olympic title as a launch pad for future success was not a new phenomenon even then. In A.D. 396 Varastades, the victor, went on to become the King of Armenia!

The light heavyweight and super heavyweight divisions have been host to some of the greatest boxers of all time. In 1984 the division that had been known as heavyweight was renamed as super heavyweight, that is, boxers over 200 lb (91 kg).

Throughout the 1960s and 1970s, boxers who wished to leave the amateur ranks used the Olympic Games as their springboard into the financially lucrative world of professional boxing. At least one champion from the light heavy or heavyweight divisions went on to become the World Professional Champion in 1960, 1964, 1968, 1972 and 1976. No doubt this was to some extent related to the growth of world interest in the Olympic

▲ Sugar Ray Leonard is one of the many boxers who have benefited financially from the sport. Leonard is now a multimillionaire.

Games. Participants in Olympic combat sports receive a great deal of publicity — an important element in boxing. By 1976 American television networks had signed up Olympic boxing stars with contracts worth over $500,000. Stars such as Sugar Ray Leonard and the Spinks brothers (Michael and Leon) benefited from these huge offers. However, we have to go back to the Helsinki Games of 1952 to find the first champion to become really rich and famous from the Olympics.

Ingemar Johansson was born in Gothenburg, Sweden, in 1932. At 6 ft (1.8 m) and 196 lb (89 kg) he was never considered a completely intimidating sight except for one detail, his right hand. Johansson said of it: "It is a gift from the gods; it is mystic and moves faster than the eye can see. I do not tell it when to go. Suddenly, boom! It lands like a thunderbolt." His punch even had a nickname — "Thor's Hammer." However, at the Games in 1952 "Thor's Hammer" was nowhere to be seen. Johansson reached the final, but was disqualified for "not giving his best" in his match against American Ed Sanders. Johansson was thrown out of the ring (there is no record of who did this) and denied his silver medal — another notorious judging "quirk." After this shaky start he got stronger and stronger while his opponent, Sanders, never produced winning form in the ring again.

In June 1959, Johansson became the World Champion when he knocked

▲ The famous Swedish boxer Ingemar Johansson was disqualified in the 1952 Olympic final in controversial circumstances.

out the American Floyd Patterson with his "mystic" right hand. In 1982 the International Olympic Committee (IOC) rewrote the record books and presented him with the silver medal that had been withheld in 1952.

The first Olympic Champion to become World Champion was Cassius Clay, or Muhammad Ali as he later preferred to be known. He won the Olympic light heavyweight title and went on to become the heavyweight World Champion. Ali was only eighteen years old when he went from his home in Louisville, Kentucky, to Rome for the 1960 Games. An enthusiastic home crowd made

▲ Muhammad Ali's career was littered with dramas and controversies. Always outspoken, he courted media attention — often to his cost.

torches out of their newspapers. The reason for their enthusiasm was the presence of six Italians competing for the ten medals. The competition began to brighten up as far as the crowd was concerned when Italian Franco De Piccoli won the heavyweight gold medal. An electrified stadium awaited the arrival of the new American boxing sensation — Ali.

Ali had made his presence felt early on by his vocal self-promotion in the Olympic village. (This behavior later became his trademark.) It was always difficult to be sure whether Ali's strenuous applauding of his own ability was honest self-belief or a media gimmick. Either way, his talent spoke for itself. Three powerful displays in the early rounds had sent clear signals to the boxing world that this was a young man to meet outside the ring, not inside.

In the light heavyweight final, Ali stepped into the ring with Zbigniew Pietrzykowski, a Polish veteran of 231 fights who had won the European championships three times. In the first round Ali's inexperience showed, and he found it difficult to score points against the confident Pietrzykowski. At the end of the second round, realizing that his relaxed style would not work, Ali changed his tactics. He was soon rewarded by connecting four punches to his opponent's head. The round saw the Pole severely rattled and the American boxing more tightly than he had before. Ali could not knock his opponent down, but he had done more than enough to win.

The story of his life after winning the Olympic gold medal is well documented. The great fights, the wins, losses and incredible comebacks, the "showbiz" sparkle, wit and personality make fascinating reading. The decline into the effects of Parkinson's Disease of this great, charismatic Olympian is a tragic yet compelling story. Ali's achievements were a milestone for black athletes. The importance of his Olympic gold medal is sometimes forgotten. Ali felt proud that he had won the medal but faced mixed reactions from fellow

Americans who preferred to patronize him as a black man in a white-dominated world. His pride for his country was short-lived when he realized just how little it was really

▲ The winner of the Olympic light heavy-weight title in Rome in 1960 proved to be one of the most famous boxers in the history of the sport. Cassius Clay (Muhammad Ali) is photographed here at the Olympic medal ceremony.

proud of him. Turning professional soon afterward allowed him to forget all national considerations. Now he could be a patriot once more — a patriot for black people.

In the Olympic years of 1964 in Tokyo and 1968 in Mexico City, two more great heavyweight stars appeared, Joe Frazier and George Foreman. Joe Frazier, later known as "Smokin' Joe," was born in Beaufort, South Carolina, in 1944. He was the seventh son of a family of thirteen children. His hero was Joe Louis, who had a similar upbringing before becoming the World Champion. To emulate his hero, Frazier filled old turnip sacks with moss and hung them from trees as makeshift punchbags. He went to Philadelphia to work in a slaughterhouse and began to box more seriously. He was only defeated in two out of forty amateur contests by Buster Mathis. In the second of the two, an Olympic trial, Mathis' victory came at the expense of a broken knuckle. This meant that

▲ Joe Frazier (left) and George Foreman, winners of the Olympic heavyweight titles in 1964 and 1968 respectively.

▶ Muhammad Ali, the great showman of boxing, defends his world heavyweight title against Britain's Joe Bugner.

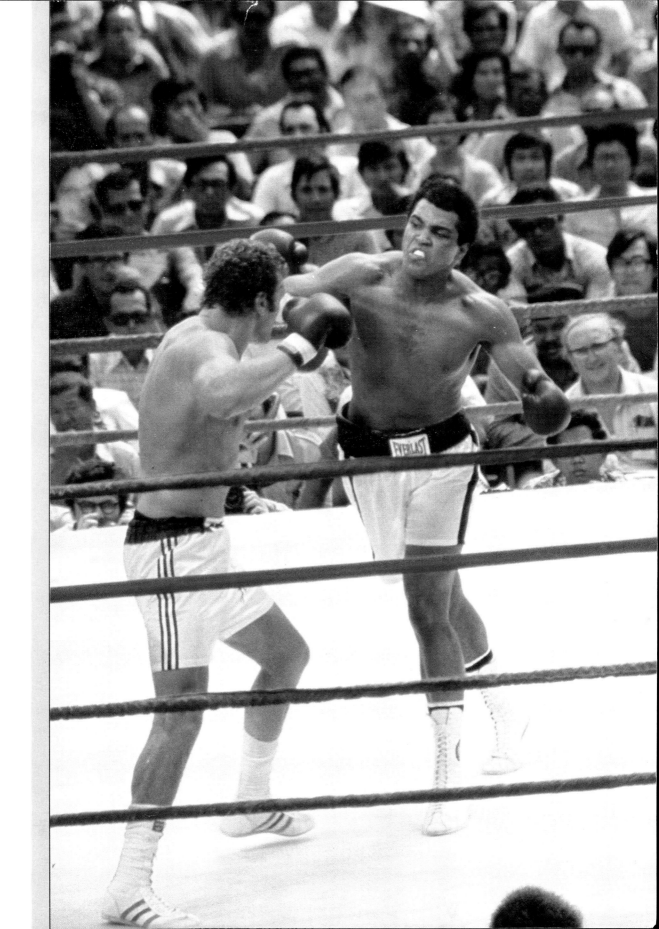

Frazier represented the United States in the Olympic heavyweight contest.

Frazier was unstoppable in Tokyo in 1964, winning the final against Hans Huber of Germany. The Tokyo Games were almost the last trouble-free Olympics. This was reflected in their "Happy Games" nickname. On returning home after the Games, the new heavyweight champion found that he had his own problems, namely a broken hand that had to be put in a cast. After the attention and glory of the Olympic Games, Frazier found himself down in the dumps with no job and no chance of fighting. He had a family to look after as well as himself. When his plight became known, the local community in Philadelphia

▲ The three faces of heavyweight boxing in the 1960s and 1970s. From left to right: Joe Frazier, George Foreman and Muhammad Ali.

stepped in to help. By the following summer Frazier was back on his feet. He turned professional, and within five years he was the World Champion.

Four years later in the altitude of Mexico City another heavyweight star came to the fore — George Foreman. He was born in 1948 in Marshall, Texas, the fifth of seven children. After leaving school at fourteen he joined rough street gangs in his neighborhood. He was encouraged to join the Job Corps, an agency designed to give young people job opportunities. In Foreman's case he was given the best opportunity

of all when in the winter of 1966, at the age of eighteen, he was encouraged to try boxing. Soon his dedication combined with his immense strength set him apart as *the* outstanding amateur boxer. He was chosen for the Olympics in Mexico City in 1968 although he had only eighteen fights behind him. Foreman dealt easily with his opponents, but in that year the media proved the most critical opponent of all. The Black Power salutes made by 200-m sprinters Tommie Smith and John Carlos from the victory platform resulted in both athletes being expelled from the U.S. Olympic squad and sent home.

Foreman's response to his victory was quite different. Perhaps with a view to his commercial future he unfurled a small Stars and Stripes from his pocket, waved it, and in those

▲ George Foreman (right) won the Olympic final in 1968 against the Soviet Iones Chapulis.

▲ A proud American! Foreman parades around the ring after his Olympic victory.

controversial Olympic Games won himself a lot of fans back home. He was quickly signed up by professional boxing promoters, and a fight was arranged with fellow Olympian Joe Frazier in 1973. Foreman was placed at 3−1 against winning the heavyweight title. But he won that fight and became the heavyweight World Champion. Foreman held the title until Muhammad Ali knocked him out in October of the following year. The influence of Ali, Frazier and Foreman still lingers, and they continue to rank among the greats in the boxing world.

In 1976 in Montreal, Canada, Michael and Leon Spinks became the first brothers in Olympic boxing history to win Olympic gold medals, Leon as a

▲ Leon Spinks (left) won the light heavyweight gold medal at the Montreal Games in 1976.

light heavyweight and Michael as a middleweight. Leon Spinks, a lance corporal in the U.S. Marine Corps, beat his Cuban opponent, Sixto Soria, comprehensively in the final. Spinks turned professional the day after he received his gold medal. Two years later Spinks beat a sadly out-of-shape Muhammad Ali to win the world heavyweight title. He held it only from February to September when he was beaten in a rematch. Michael Spinks stepped up from middleweight to heavyweight not long after his Olympic victory in 1976. Many Olympic boxers fight in lower weight categories before moving up when they turn professional. So Michael was not an exception.

In the middleweight competition in 1976, Michael Spinks had to face Riskiev of the Soviet Union who had beaten him six months earlier. Michael had an easy route to the final thanks to one bye (when his opponent failed to turn up) and two forfeits. As expected, the American faced the Soviet boxer in the final. All looked fairly evenly matched until they reached the final round when Spinks hit his opponent with a mighty body blow. The referee had to step in and stop the distressed Soviet from receiving any more punishment. Michael had a very different

▲ Like his brother Leon, Michael Spinks chose to fight professionally as a heavyweight.

▼ Michael Spinks (right) won the middleweight title in Montreal. He stepped up to heavyweight and became the World Champion.

attitude to the professional scene to that of his brother Leon. Michael said: "I couldn't stand to see another person living comfortably by jerking me out of my money. Treating me like a horse or cow. It was too vicious." Although he did turn professional, Michael made sure that he was never exploited in the same way as Leon, along with countless other fighters, was by so-called advisors.

Michael Spinks did become the heavyweight World Champion. However, in the defense of his title he was unfortunate to come up against the lethal Mike Tyson. Fellow American Tyson beat him to become the undisputed World Champion. Tyson never fought at the Olympics, he always claimed that the Amateur Boxing Association (ABA) was prejudiced against him. Tyson was the most famous heavyweight champion never to box at the Olympics.

The most successful boxer in Olympic history is triple gold medalist Teofilo Stevenson of Cuba. He is not nearly as famous as any other gold medalist of recent times for the simple reason that he never became a professional. This fact, of course, allowed him to box on in the Olympics to win more medals than usual. His first win came in Munich in 1972. The Munich Games are associated with one of the worst tragedies in the history of sports. Palestinian terrorists broke into the Olympic village and held nine members of the Israeli team as

▲ Teofilo Stevenson of Cuba acknowledges the crowd after winning one of his three Olympic heavyweight gold medals.

hostages. Later, at the airport, all nine hostages, five of the terrorists and a police officer were killed during a rescue attempt. The Games continued in an atmosphere of terrible sorrow.

In 1972 the heavyweight gold medal was estimated to be worth $1,000,000 to the winner — probably more if that winner had been Duane David Bobick. Bobick had an outstanding amateur record and went to

▶ The statuesque Stevenson (right) taunts his opponent before delivering a contest-winning blow.

the Games as the great hope of the United States. The only fighter to have upset him at all had been Teofilo Stevenson in the Pan-American Games. In the first round Nesterov of the Soviet Union hurt Bobick around the eyes, an injury that later proved decisive. Stevenson took little punishment from Denderys of Poland, whom he dispatched in just over a minute.

When Bobick and Stevenson stepped into the ring together in the quarter-final the atmosphere was electric. The prospect of the elegant Stevenson fighting the tough Bobick was very exciting. In the past, the Cuban boxer had been criticized for his weak right hand. He had trained and worked extremely hard to strengthen it. The damage around Bobick's left eye was the perfect target for Stevenson's invigorated right hand. Bobick attacked furiously from the outset, sending hard punches to his opponent's body. All the time Stevenson withstood the pressure while peppering Bobick's bad eye with punches. This turned out to be an effective tactic. Bobick's eye puffed up so badly that he could hardly see. The referee was forced to stop the fight near the beginning of the third round.

In the semifinal Stevenson faced local hero, Peter Hussing of Germany. The Cuban quickly found a way through Hussing's defense with his right hand. He pounded the German's chin, and the referee had to stop the fight. His opponent for the final, Ion Alexe of Romania, broke a thumb and

In the heavyweight final in Montreal, Stevenson was taken to three rounds by Mircea Simon of Romania.

had to concede. With Stevenson's hand working in the way it had done in the early rounds, Alexe would seem to have gotten off easily.

Stevenson, coming from a country that outlawed professional boxing, was not tempted by lucrative financial offers. He said: ''Professional boxing treats a fighter like a commodity to be bought and sold and discarded when he is no longer of any use.'' His words have proved to have had more than a ring of truth.

Stevenson returned to the Olympics in Montreal four years later. In the meantime he had been beaten only twice, both times by the Soviet Igor Vysotsky, who was unable to fight in the Games because of eye injuries. Stevenson's first three fights took a total of eight minutes, with all three lasting, on average, less than one round. In the final, his opponent, Mircea Simon of Romania, danced around the ring to try to avoid the fate of the Cuban's other opponents. Stevenson finally managed to catch up with the Romanian in the third round.

Fearful of their boxer's fate, Simon's corner men threw the white towel of surrender into the ring.

Four years later in Moscow, Stevenson fought for yet another Olympic title. Because of the boycott of the Games by the United States and some West European countries, the

▼ In Moscow in 1980, Stevenson won his third Olympic title. The brilliant Cuban boxer received many lucrative offers to turn professional but chose to remain an amateur.

tournament was somewhat depleted. (The boycott was a protest against the Soviet Union's invasion of Afghanistan.) For the first time, Stevenson was forced to go the distance by Istvan Levai in the semi-final. The 6 ft 2 in (1.88 m) champion could barely land his punches, his twenty-nine years weighing heavily upon him. In the end the judges awarded Stevenson victory against his tenth Olympic opponent. It has been remarked that Levai's delight at survival (after all, he lost the fight) was like that of a man winning a gold medal — such was the esteem in which Stevenson was universally held. In the final he faced Pyotr Zaev. The Soviet boxer could not prevent the tall Cuban from winning and becoming the first

man to win three Olympic boxing gold medals in the same weight division. The great Laszlo Papp won three golds, but in different divisions. It must be remembered that Stevenson never had to fight the very best heavyweights, except in 1972. However, this should not detract from his powerful punching and deep commitment to the ideals of the Olympic Games.

The Munich Games proved a tremendous occasion for other Cuban boxers. Cuba was the most successful nation in the tournament. The United States had a disastrous time and won only one title. Cuba's successes were in the bantamweight, won by Orlando Martinez, the welterweight, where the aggressive Emilio Correa triumphed, and the heavyweight, won by Teofilo Stevenson.

Martinez beat George Turpin of Great Britain and then Alfonso Zamora of Mexico in the final to become Cuba's first Olympic gold medalist since Ramon Forst, who won a gold for fencing in 1904. Martinez was soon joined on the winner's rostrum by Stevenson later the same day. The following day the nineteen-year-old Pan-American Champion Emilio Correa fought the thirty-two-year-old Hungarian Janos Kajdi in the welterweight division. Correa's victory gave Cuba its third gold medal in two days.

◀ Lennox Lewis of Canada pins Riddick Bowe to the ropes before winning the super heavyweight contest in Seoul in 1988.

PAPP

L aszlo Papp was born in Budapest, Hungary, in 1926. In 1948 he traveled to London to box in the middleweight division at the Olympic Games. He later claimed that his victory over the British fighter John Wright was his hardest fight. No doubt the partisan crowd inspired Wright. The British boxer failed to make any impact on the boxing scene afterward.

The 1952 Games were held in Helsinki, Finland. These Olympics were known as the "Friendly Games," because they were the first since World War II where all countries participated. The introduction of two new divisions — light middleweight and light welterweight — allowed Papp to drop down a division, to light middleweight, where his weight was evenly matched with the other fighters. In one of the first rounds he fought Ellsworth "Spider" Webb. Spider knocked out World Champions such as Joey Giardello and Terry Downes later in his career. However, he was no match for Papp at the peak of the Hungarian's powers. In the final, Papp had a tough bout with Theunis van Schalkwyk from South Africa. Papp's strongest opponent yet in this tournament held him at bay for the first two rounds until a thundering right hook knocked van Schalkwyk to the ground.

At the next Olympics in Melbourne, Australia, Papp was still eligible to compete because he had remained an amateur. This was as much through his government's intervention as through his own wishes. The circumstances were not the easiest for the boxer to

▲ Laszlo Papp of Hungary won the middleweight title in 1948 in London and the light middleweight titles in 1952 and 1956.

▲ Papp had a brilliant Olympic career. Not only did he win three boxing titles, but after retiring from the professional scene in 1965 he became Hungary's official Olympic boxing coach.

seek his third gold medal. Hungary was still in revolt against the Soviet regime, and the Hungarian athletes were forced to hide in the cellar of a Budapest hotel before they could make their way to Melbourne. There they received the biggest cheer from the crowd at the opening day ceremonies. The cheers must have rung particularly loudly for Papp. In Melbourne, he had to beat the toughest opponents to win his third gold medal. First he overcame Zbigniew Pietrzykowski, a formidable

Polish fighter who was to give Muhammad Ali some problems four years later.

The sympathy of the crowd for the Hungarian people's fate supported the fighter in the hard-fought bouts. The hardest of these was without doubt the fight against José Torres in the final. The formidable Torres was born in Puerto Rico but represented the United States. The first round went the American's way, his left hand finding gaps in Papp's defense. In the second round Papp hit Torres with a mighty left hook to the jaw, which sent the American onto the ropes. According to reports, ''the packs of Hungarian supporters nearly lifted the roof off the stadium,'' with their shouts of joy. After the cautious third and final round, the judges gave the decision in Papp's favor. The celebrations continued long after the fight was over. The defeated Torres went on to win the world light-weight championship and in retirement became the chairperson of the New York State Athletic Commission. The Hungarian government allowed Papp to turn professional in the following year at the age of thirty-one.

Papp was the first boxer from a communist country to fight pro-fessionally. He won the European championship but was denied a shot at the world title by the Hungarian government. He was undefeated when he retired in 1965 and went on to become Hungary's official Olympic boxing coach.

FENCING

The popularity of fencing in the nineteenth century ensured its inclusion in the very first Olympics of the modern era in Athens in 1896. There are three different blades used: the foil, épée and saber. The foil has a flexible rectangular blade and a blunt point. Touches from its point alone must be made on the trunk between the collar bone and the hip. The épée is rigid, and touches with its point on any part of the body count. This is because of its origin as a dueling weapon. The saber is a flexible triangular blade; all of its sides may be used to make touches on the body above the waist. This is because it was originally a cavalry weapon. Women fight only with the foil.

At the first two Olympic celebrations, in 1896 in Athens and in 1900 in Paris, both amateurs and professionals competed for honors. The professionals were excluded after 1900. Team events were first held in 1904 in St. Louis, and they have run side-by-side with the individual events ever since. As with gymnastics, fencers enter many events. This has meant that some fencers have won several medals at one Games.

 An individual foil contest in Seoul in 1988.

The first of the multi-medalists was the Italian Nedo Nadi. Nadi, born in 1893, was brought up in a sporting environment where he was taught to use the foil when he was very young. By the age of fifteen he could handle the other swords, too. He was competing in international competitions by 1911. The following year at the Games in Stockholm, Sweden, Nedo won the foil competition by the largest of margins. Although only eighteen years old, he displayed such skill that many considered his the best fencing performance in the Olympics. This was a considerable achievement since fencing is the one sport where age is expected to improve a player's performance. World War I meant that the scheduled 1916 Olympic Games did not take place. The next Games were in 1920 in Antwerp. It was here that Nedo produced a supremely masterful performance by winning the individual gold medals in foil and saber and gold medals in the team category for the foil, saber and épée. His contribution to the team gold in the épée is remarkable because his father, also his instructor, disapproved of it to the point of excluding it from his gymnasium. When or where Nedo ever had the chance to practice the épée is not known. Aldo Nadi, Nedo's younger

▲ G. Nostini of Italy (left) in a fencing duel with A. Aszlay of Hungary in the foil competition in 1948 in London.

▶ Fencing appears to be a violent sport. Combatants wear protective padding, but occasionally injuries occur.

brother, fought on the same teams and picked up three gold medals, a considerable family accomplishment.

The length of time that fencers remain in Olympic competition is quite unusual. Aladar Gerevich won gold medals at six consecutive Olympic Games, and Ivan Osiier's Olympic career spanned forty years. Osiier's experience was not much help; he won only one silver medal, in 1912. He might be known as the most persistent of all Olympians.

Fencing is a little difficult to follow because of the speed of the blades. Sometimes even judges find it hard to tell whether a hit has been made or not.

▲ Helsinki in 1952 — winner of the men's individual foil title, Christian d'Oriola (center), and the silver and bronze medalists.

To help them, electric scoring equipment was introduced for the épée in 1936 in Berlin and for the foil in 1956 in Melbourne. With the new system, a light flashes if the fencer hits the designated area. The introduction of the electric equipment, particularly in 1956, had a profound effect on the sport. Now that fencers no longer had to be seen to make hits, their speed increased and their style declined. The great stylist Christian d'Oriola, winner of two individual foil medals, retired

▲ French fencer Christian d'Oriola (right) in full combative action at the 1948 Olympic Games in London.

after these Games, knowing that his style of fencing was going to disappear. The appearance of the Soviet team introduced a new, more athletic form of fencing, and an end to the more classical era. Today, the dominant countries in fencing are France, Italy, the Soviet Union and Hungary.

The Games in 1956 witnessed one of fencing's greatest upsets and arguably Britain's most unexpected medal. At the last moment the British

Olympic appeal fund raised enough money to send a woman fencer; Gillian Sheen was chosen. Sheen was the undisputed British champion, though her previous international performances were undistinguished. It was assumed that the new, heavier electric foils would put her at a disadvantage. But her experience showed, and she quickly adapted to the new weapon. The first round saw the French and Soviet champions defeated. A fence-off with Hungary's champion, Lydia Domilki, got Sheen through to the last round. In the final, she tied with the Romanian Olga Orban. In the fence-off for the gold medal, the British fencer mounted a quick attack that saw her take a 3−1 lead. The Romanian could pull back only one point before Sheen finished the match 4−2. It was Britain's first fencing gold. Gillian Sheen's victory was so totally un-expected that there were no British reporters on hand to record it. The news was telexed back to her proud parents in England.

▶ Olympic fencer and undisputed British champion Gillian Sheen sets off for the 1956 Games in Melbourne.

▼ Gillian Sheen (left) competing against R. Garilhe of France in the women's individual foil event in Melbourne. Sheen caused a major upset by winning the gold medal.

JUDO

Judo first became an Olympic sport in Tokyo in 1964. This was hardly surprising since the sport originated there a century earlier. It was the only martial art to have received Olympic recognition until taekwondo was included as a demonstration sport in Barcelona in 1992. Judo teaches self-defense as well as a whole philosophy of behavior — the word judo means ''the gentle way.''

Judo was founded by Jigoro Kano. He conceived of an activity that would be related purely to skill, rather than weight or strength. In fact, until 1984, there was an Olympic open category where fighters of all weights could compete. However, this was becoming a second heavyweight division because

▼ The ''Flying Dutchman,'' Anton Geesink, throws his opponent to the floor in Tokyo in 1964. Geesink won the open category title.

the techniques of the larger fighters increasingly kept up the weight levels. To counter this, entry to both events by any one fighter was prevented in Los Angeles in 1984. Gone too is the resemblance to anything remotely gentle. The gentle qualities or attributes are hardly apparent in modern judo bouts — in much the same way that the Olympic philosophy is sometimes forgotten in the heat of competition. This is probably due to the growing popularity of judo in the West as a competitive sport rather than a philosophy.

When it was first contested in 1964, only four categories were included: lightweight, middleweight, heavy-weight and open. The first Japanese victor was Isao Okano. He won the middleweight division after a particularly harrowing experience in the quarter-finals against Frenchman Lionel Grossain. Grossain lost consciousness while in a hold, and Okano had to revive him. The Japanese took three golds in all. However, the victory by Anton Geesink of the Netherlands in the most prestigious category, the open, was an ominous blow to the Japanese.

Geesink was born in Utrecht in 1934. He grew to a mammoth 6 ft 6 in (1.98 m) and weighed 266 lb (121 kg). He took his world title in 1961, after five attempts, thanks to his ability to combine his huge size with lightning movement. In Tokyo he faced his arch opponent, Akio Kaminga, whom he

▲ Willem Ruska of the Netherlands celebrates after defeating German Klaus Glahn to win the judo heavyweight gold medal in 1972. He also won the open title at the Games.

had beaten in the quarter-final in the 1961 world championship. Geesink had won his semifinal bout in only 12 seconds, so his confidence was running high. He defeated Kamingo easily. It was a significant moment for the Japanese. The masters now found that their pupils were teaching them some unforgettable lessons!

Judo was not included in the Olympic program in 1968 in Mexico City. It returned in 1972 at Munich with two more categories, light middle-weight and light heavyweight. This time the Japanese lost out in the three heavier divisions. The main architect of their downfall was Willem Ruska of the Netherlands. He was the first man to win in two categories—heavyweight and open. Though the Japanese were dominant in the lighter divisions, they seemed to be losing their grip on the very sport they had been instrumental in bringing to the Games.

The Olympic year of 1980 was very frustrating for the Japanese. They did not attend the Games along with the United States to protest against the Soviet invasion of Afghanistan. The U.S. boycott was also followed by Canada, West Germany, Kenya, Norway, Israel and Turkey. Some athletes from other countries decided on individual boycotts. For other nations it was no doubt good news, though people at the top of their sport prefer to fight against the best to win their titles, rather than win them by default.

The most extraordinary contest was for the lightweight title, between Ezio Gamba of Italy and Neil Adams of Great Britain. With the absence of the Japanese, Adams and Gamba were the main medal favorites. Gamba, incidentally, was the only Italian judo combatant at the Games. The other Italian competitors were in the Italian army and, therefore, subject to their government's boycott.

In the semifinal, Adams faced Karl-Heinz Lehmann of Germany — his most feared opponent. Adams won the match easily, in contrast to Gamba's

▼ Neil Adams of Britain battles with Karl-Heinz Lehmann of Germany in a lightweight semifinal contest in 1980 in Moscow. Adams won this bout but lost the final.

harder route to the final. However, youth and inexperience told as Adams stepped off the mat after the semifinal fully expecting the final to begin immediately. However, he had five hours to wait. During that time his motivation slipped. He became complacent, for he had beaten Gamba in every final he had ever fought. When Adams got to the mat, his "touch" was gone. He was slow and badly organized against a man he could have beaten, and had beaten in the past nine times out of ten. Adams' confidence somehow left him, and soon Gamba was winning the bout, much to Adams' horror and disbelief. The bell went and with it the gold for Adams, as the decision went to Gamba. Adams wrote afterward: "It was the loneliest moment of my entire life. I didn't know what to do, I just felt sick. I also remember thinking, 'They've made a mistake. They are going to reverse the decision any moment.' But of course, it never happened. I stood on the mat watching the commotion that surrounded Gamba, completely numbed and lost for words."

In 1981 Adams compensated for this loss in the world championships. Victory in the semifinals meant he was

▼ Adams of Great Britain and Alksnim of Poland in a strange combination in 1980. Adams was devastated at failing to win the gold medal.

the first Briton to reach the finals of that competition. In the final he beat Jiro Kase of Japan, thanks to a powerful arm lock.

The boycott, and consequent non-participation of the Japanese in 1980, was particularly upsetting for Japan's judo fans because of the emergence of their greatest star. Yasuhiro Yamashita was considered *the* person who would rekindle Japan's pride in the sport. Yamashita was 5 ft 11 in (1.8 m) tall and weighed 280 lb (127 kg). He began to display his star quality in 1977, and coming up to the Moscow Games he was easily the favorite. The boycott meant that his unbeaten record would not result in an Olympic medal. He had countless offers to turn professional and become a *sumo* wrestler, but he resisted them all. All Yamashita wanted was to stand on the highest step of the victory podium at the Olympic Games.

So, four years later, the Los Angeles Games had a particular significance for one man and his country. These Games were also affected by a boycott. This time it was the turn of the East European countries (except for Romania). They claimed that their boycott was in protest against the security arrangements and the capitalist approach. Many felt it was in retaliation for the 1980 boycott. For the record, Yamashita was unbeaten from 1977 in 194 contests. He won the world championships three times and was champion of Japan eight times. During the four-year period between

▲ The great Japanese hope for Olympic judo glory, Yasuhiro Yamashita. The boycott of the Moscow Games delayed his dream.

the Moscow and Los Angeles Games — a period known as the Olympiad — it was decided to prevent fighters from entering both heavyweight and open categories. This removed the possibility that Yamashita would have two bites at the cherry.

The Judo competitions were held in the gymnasium of the California State University in Los Angeles. On the day of the final rounds 4,000 spectators watched three Japanese win in lower weight categories, but the world was waiting to see Yamashita. Things were not going as smoothly as hoped or expected for Yamashita. In his first round match against Schnabel of West Germany, he dominated his opponent but in doing so received an injury in his right leg. The injury was bad enough to make him limp. Two hours later in the semifinal, his opponent, Delcolumbo, attacked Yamashita's bad leg. This is considered a perfectly fair strategy in judo, and one that Yamashita admitted he would have used himself if the roles had been reversed. But this time the strategy did not pay off. Delcolumbo was unbalanced in his attack. Yamashita seized upon this, threw and held his opponent for victory and a place in the Olympic final.

The other finalist was the formidable Rashwan of Egypt. Rashwan progressed to the final by beating each of his opponents with an ippon — the full point (worth ten small points) awarded for a perfectly executed throw. It was a different scenario with Yamashita. The final lasted only a few seconds, with the Japanese master finding little opposition to his determined assault on the Olympic title. The big, powerful victor stood and bowed at his defeated opponent in the traditional manner. Tears welled in his eyes as he limped off to celebrate with his teammates. They, in turn, did something no opponent in judo could ever do — they swept him off his feet and threw him in the air in jubilation. At last Yamashita had won the medal he had so obviously deserved but had to wait to win. Few competitors affected by the boycott were as persistent as Yamashita. Perhaps only Edwin Moses, the 400-m hurdler, came through the boycotts relatively unscarred.

Los Angeles also saw the continuing saga of Neil Adam's search for gold. This time he had a more taxing route to the final. He had to face Brett Barron of

 Yamashita gives a demonstration of his superior strength. In 1984 in Los Angeles, the Japanese judo hero fulfilled his ambition to win an Olympic heavyweight judo gold medal.

the United States in the second round. The partisan crowd and the fear of biased judging provoked Adams. He managed to get his opponent on the ground and snapped on an arm lock. Barron immediately submitted. This was not surprising because Adams had been so vigorous in the move that he had actually dislocated and fractured Barron's elbow. When he met Barron in the Olympic village the next day, Adams apologized and offered to sign the cast. It must be only in Japanese that the word judo means "the gentle way!"

In the final Adams faced Wienecke of West Germany, again someone he had beaten previously. His motivation against an opponent who appeared much weaker than himself was dubious. Adams assumed victory was his. He subsequently admitted that during the contest he actually looked at the clock and thought: "Three minutes to go and you're Olympic Champion." Suddenly, the two contestants were so close to the edge of the mat that Adams was expecting nothing. Wienecke went for a left shoulder throw — ippon-seoinage. This throw, if well executed, is awarded ten contest-winning points. Adams hit the mat and thought that he would have a waza-ari — seven points — awarded against him.

To his amazement and horror a full ippon was signaled. The match was over and another gold had slipped from his grasp. What was even more astonishing was that throughout his twenty years of judo Adams had never once been thrown for a full ippon! Now in an Olympic final with a gold medal at stake, Adams had fallen for what, in another sport, would be called a "sucker" punch.

▲ Neil Adams lost the 1984 Los Angeles lightweight final to Frank Wieneke of Germany (right).

Women's judo was included in the 1988 Games in Seoul as a demonstration sport. The standard was so high and the competition was so intense that women's judo was officially recognized as an Olympic sport in 1992 in Barcelona.

WRESTLING

Wrestling is such a universal activity that most countries around the world have one or more versions of it. There is *sumo* in Japan, *sambo* in the Soviet Union, *yagli* in Turkey and *glima* in Iceland. In Britain there are many styles: *Cumberland, Westmoreland, Devonshire* and *Cornwall* among others.

The Olympic freestyle category allows a wide range of attacks. The wrestlers can use their legs and arms to throw, trip and sweep their opponents to the ground. There they must pin their opponents' shoulders to the ground for a clear second for victory. The Greco-Roman style is a purer form of wrestling. It forbids holds below the hips or use of the legs in any attacking way. This forces the contestants to try to unbalance their opponents. To its detriment, Greco-Roman wrestling is not as exciting to watch (for the uninitiated). The flowing freestyle contest is more popular.

Amateur wrestling is quite unlike professional wrestling. Amateurs are

▲ The immense figure of a *sumo* wrestler. *Sumo* is the traditional form of wrestling in Japan.

not allowed to kick or punch, or apply holds that endanger life or limb. The arm locks and strangleholds that are a well-established part of everyday professional contests are forbidden.

Wrestling was one of the first sports in the original Olympic Games. It has remained a part of the Olympic movement since 776 B.C. It was revived

▲ *Sambo* wrestling originated in the Soviet Union where it is still hugely popular. Here it is demonstrated by two women combatants.

as part of the modern Olympics at the first of the new Games in Athens in 1896, but only in the Greco-Roman style. The single contested category was the open division. Its victor, Karl Schumann of Germany, also won medals in gymnastic events — the long horse vault, the team parallel bars and the horizontal bars.

Eight years later in St. Louis the only competitors were American. The freestyle category was introduced at these Games. Originally there were no time limits on the bouts so that contestants could keep going until they

◀ Note the powerful and muscular physique of wrestler S. V. Bacon who represented Britain and Ireland at the 1908 Games in London.

▼ N. Akkar, ''The Terrible Turk,'' holds Kouyos of France down in a wrestling bantamweight contest at the 1948 Games.

▲ Atan of Turkey swings Kangasniemi of Finland around during the heavyweight wrestling finals in Helsinki in 1952.

overwhelmed their opponents. This often led to extremely long contests. The most extreme of all contests took place in Stockholm in 1912. The middleweight Greco-Roman contest was between Martin Klein from Estonia in the Soviet Union and Alfred "Alpo" Asikainen from Finland. The contest was evenly matched, but eventually it proved almost too evenly matched and neither contestant could get an advantage. Soon they started taking half-hourly refreshment breaks! Klein eventually prevailed — eleven hours later. He was so exhausted that he was unable to compete in the final

and settled for the silver medal. In the light heavyweight division in Stockholm, the wrestlers in the final, Anders Ahlgren of Sweden and Ivar Bohling of Finland, were level after nine hours, so they were declared equal second. Luckily, the rules were changed, and bouts took place in three 2-minute rounds — quite a change!

The first great Olympic wrestling star was Carl Westergren of Sweden. He was born in Malmo in 1895 and

▲ Aleksandr Medved (in the red) is considered the greatest modern wrestler. He won three consecutive Olympic gold medals.

▼ Chris Taylor of the United States (top) wrestles with Yorihide Isogai of Japan in 1972 in Munich.

began wrestling in 1911. In 1920 in Antwerp he won his first Olympic gold medal with victory in the Greco-Roman middleweight competition. Two years later he became the World Champion. In Paris in 1924 he won the equivalent of the light heavyweight division. Four years later he went to Amsterdam in search of a third consecutive title. Unfortunately he lost in the first round to Onni Pellinen, who went on to win the bronze. So Westergren had to wait a further four years for a shot at a record third title. He went to Los Angeles in 1932 at the age of thirty-six and swept all opposition before him to win the gold.

Kustaa Pihlajamaki of Finland is another great Olympic wrestler. He came from a family of wrestlers and was tough as well as very quick. Wrestling experts consider him the best lightweight wrestler of all time. He also won three gold medals, in 1924, 1932 and 1936, as well as a silver in 1928. He was such a hero in his own country that a monument was built in his honor in Helsinki, the capital of Finland.

The greatest modern wrestler was without doubt Aleksandr Medved. Medved was born in the Ukraine in the Soviet Union in 1937. His consistency was amazing. Between 1964 and 1972 he won three successive Olympic titles, and he was World Champion each year except for 1965. He was a fantastic fighter, able to beat wrestlers who were often as much as 140 lb (64 kg) heavier than him. In this respect he surpassed himself in 1972 in Munich when faced with Chris Taylor from the United States. Taylor was almost twice the Soviet's weight. They met in the first round and Taylor was penalized for passivity! Medved's reputation was enough to intimidate even a man of Taylor's size.

▼ Surprisingly, wrestling is one of the least violent combat sports.

GLOSSARY

Boycott To stay away from somewhere or refuse to have dealings with someone or something as a protest.

Capitalism A system in which a country's land and wealth is owned mainly by individuals and not by the state.

Commodity Something useful.

Complacent Very pleased or self-satisfied.

Consecutive Following one after the other in order.

Contentious Likely to cause an argument or dispute.

Impartial Not favoring one person or team any more than another.

Intimidate To threaten someone (generally with violence) to force him or her to do something.

Invigorated To be filled with energy.

Motto A short sentence or phrase that expresses an idea.

Partisan To be devoted to someone.

Passive Not active.

Prestigious Important and highly regarded.

Scenario The summary of a plot.

Sumo The national style of wrestling in Japan. The object is to force the opponent to touch the ground with any part of his body except his feet, or to force him to step out of the ring.

Vitality Liveliness.

FURTHER READING

Frommer, Harvey. *Olympic Controversies*. New York: Franklin Watts, 1987.

Glubock, Shirley and Alfred Tamarin. *Olympic Games in Ancient Greece*. New York: Harper Junior Books, 1976.

Greenberg, Stan, ed. *The Guinness Book of Olympic Facts & Feats*. New York: Bantam, 1984.

Marshall, Nancy Thies. *Women Who Compete*. Old Tappan, N.J.: Fleming H. Revell Company, 1988.

Tatlow, Peter. *The Olympics*. New York: Franklin Watts, 19788.

Walczewski, Michael. *The Olympic Fun Fact Book*. New York: Dell, 1988.

Wallechinsky, David. *The Complete Book of the Olympics*. New York: Penguin Books, 1988.

INDEX

The numbers in **bold** refer to captions.

Adams, Neil 35, **35**, 36, **36**, 37, 38, 40, **40**
Ali, Muhammad (Cassius Clay) 11–12, **12**, 13, **13**, 14, **15**, **16**, 18, 26

Bobick, Duane David 20, 22
Boxing 4, 6–26
    bantamweight 24
    controversies 6, 7–8, 9, 10, 11
    featherweight 9
    heavyweight 10–24
    light heavyweight 10, 18
    light middleweight 25
    light welterweight 25
    middleweight 10, 18, 19
    super heavyweight 10
    welterweight 24

Combat sports
    see individual sport name

de Coubertin, Baron Pierre 4, 6
d'Oriola, Christian 30–31
Douglas, J. W. H. T. 6, **6**

Eagan, Edward 7

Fencing 4, 24, 27–32
    épée 27–28
    equipment 31
    foil 27–29
    saber 27–28
Foreman, George 14, **14**, 16, **16**, 17, **17**, 18
Frazier, Joe 14, **14**, 15, 16, **16**, 18

Gamba, Ezio 35–36
Geesink, Anton **33**, 34

Johansson, Ingemar 11, **11**
Judo 4, 33–40
    heavyweight 33, 34, 37
    light heavyweight 34
    light middleweight 34
    lightweight 34
    middleweight 34
    open 33, 34, 37

Leonard, Sugar Ray **10**, 11
Louis, Joe 14

Medved, Aleksandr **44**, 45
Motto, Olympic 4, 5, 7

Nadi, Nedo 28–30

Olympic Games
    Amsterdam 1928 9, 44–45
    Antwerp, 1920 6–8, 28, 44
    Athens, 1896 4, **5**, 27, 42
    Berlin, 1936 28, 30, 45
    Helsinki, 1952 11, 25, **30**, **43**
    London, 1908 6, **6**, **42**
    London, 1948 **8**, **9**, 24, **28**, **31**, **42**
    Los Angeles, 1932 44–45
    Los Angeles, 1984 10, 33–34, 37, **38**
    Melbourne, 1955 25–26, 28, 30–31, **32**
    Mexico City, 1968 14, 16–17, 34
    Montreal, 1976 18–19, 22–23

Moscow, 1980 23–24, 35, 37
Munich, 1972 20, 24, 34, **44**, 45
Paris, 1900 27
Paris, 1924 8, 27, 44–45
Rome, 1960 11
Seoul, 1988 7–8, **27**, 40
St. Louis, 1904 6, 10, 24, 27, 42
Stockholm, 1912 6, 28, 30, 43
Tokyo, 1964 14, 16, 33, **33**, 34

Papp, Laszlo 25, **25**, 26, **26**
Patterson, Floyd 11
Pihlajamaki, Kustaa 45

Ruska, Willem 34, **34**

Sheen, Gillian 31–32, **32**

Simon, Mircea 23
Spinks, Leon 11, 18, **18**, 20
Spinks, Michael 11, 18–19, **19**, 20
Stevenson, Teofilo 20, **20**, **21**, 22, **22**, 23, **23**,24

Taylor, Chris **44**, 45
Tyson, Mike 20

Westergren, Carl 43–45
Wrestling 4, 41–45
    Greco-Roman 41–44
    sambo 41
    sumo 41

Yamashita, Yasuhiro 37, **37**, 38, **39**